30 MYSTERY OF SUCCESS

ISU EVANGEL EWA

30

MYSTERY

OF

SUCCESS

Isu Evangel Ewa

CONTENT

3. SMILE ALWAYS

4. MAKE PLANS

5. SET TARGET(GOALS)

6. TAKE ACTION

7. BE SOCIAL

8. BE NICE TO PEOPLE

9. BE YOURSELF

10. LOVE YOURSELF

11. LOVE WHAT YOU DO (PASSION)

12. LEARN TO FORGIVE

13. HAVE FUN

14. GIVE TO PEOPLE

15. VALUE CORRECTION

16. NEVER PROMISE WHAT YOU WON'T DO

17. DON'T SPEND EXTRAVAGANTLY

18. READ A LOT

19. LOVE TRAVEL

20.   USE THE LUR FORMULAR

21.   BE COMMITTED

22.   SEEK ADVICE FROM RESPONSIBLE PEOPLE

23.   X-RAY YOUR BEHAVIOR

24.   STOP THE BLAME

25.   PUT OUT FEAR

26. BE SACRIFICIAL

27. GET A MENTOR

28. WORRY LESS

29. BE CONSISTENT

30. PRAY FERVENTLY

Everybody wants to be successful. You want to wear nice clothes, get a well paying job, live in a well furnished apartment, buy expensive things and so on. But the truth is, not everyone who wishes to be successful would end up as a successful person. To some, it will be a mere wish that would never happen and to others it would be a dream come true, or perhaps a wish come true.

Becoming a successful person is not a day job. One would not wake up from slumber saying he wants to be successful and it happens immediately. Success is a gradual process.

But do you know that there are some mysteries about success which many do not know. It takes more than hardwork to attain success. A lot of people work hard all day, struggling to meet their needs and yet they are not making success.

In this book, I unveiled 30 mystery which can make you successful in all your endeavours. So after reading and practicing what is in this book and your life do not change for good, then I must say your case is spiritual.

Study this book, practice what is written therein and watch yourself soar higher. I wish you happy reading.

1. FORGET THE PAST

Its hard for one to forget some events that happened in the past. As far as you are a human being, every event that happens in your life is stored in your brain.

By forgetting the past, that is forgetting every incidence that happened in your life causing a negative effect on you.

Do not bring the past into the present else it will affect the future. Successful people bury their past because the past can hinder their progress in the present and in future.

2. THINK BEFORE YOU ACT

This is another mystery which makes people successful. You need to think before you take any action.

 In thinking before acting, you need to consider the advantages and the disadvantages of the action. If the advantage is more than the disadvantages, go ahead with the plan. But if the disadvantages is greater than the advantages, then forget about it.

4. SMILE ALWAYS

Do you know that smiling everyday would attribute to your success? It is a mystery of becoming successful. Never cease to smile even if someone offends you. Get angry but don't over do it.

When you smile all day, you'll surely put your enemies into total disarray.

5. MAKE PLANS

You can never be successful if you don't make plans. You need to plan your life, plan your future and shape them.

Design your future and turn them into reality. As an architect draw the plan of a house before further construction, so should you always plan your life.

5. SET TARGET (GOALS)

Yes. This is one of the crucial mystery of success. Let's take an eagle as a case study.

 An eagle a bird known for setting targets. Each time it sees a prey, it will first target its prey to know when to strike and whenever he strikes, he'll surely catch that prey.

Set targets or goals in your business. List all the goals you want to achieve in a particular year ,month, week or even day. Work towards them and make sure you complete at least 60% of the goals listed.

6. TAKE ACTION

Just like one of my coach, **Favour Joseph (the mindset engineer)** said "... You can never achieve what you have never achieved before unless you take actions you have not taken before". This is very true.

A student who wishes to score a very high grade in an exam will never succeed unless he studies more than he used to.

Action begat result. You can only get a desired result when you take a desired action. So, start now to take actions if you want to succeed.

7. BE SOCIAL

You got to be social if you really want to be successful. Being social is one of the tools for greater achievements.

 Make friends with good people, associate yourself with different kinds of people — people of different races, tribes , ages , ethnicity and the rest not mentioned.

8. BE NICE TO PEOPLE

"Be nice to people on your way up because you may need them on your way down "

The above quote is nothing new to anybody. It is something I hear everyday and it's true. Treat people the way you want them to treat you. Don't be so naive that you forget the existence of the laws of karma — what goes around comes around.

Even your old friends are important. You'll need their help one day. Just be nice to people and see how far you'll go in life.

9. BE YOURSELF

You've always wanted to be like the top musicians, you've always wanted to be an influential writer, you've always wanted to be seen as the best actor or actress, but you are not always yourself.

You try to copy others and still nothing works out. Take it easy, look beyond the walls and do things originally in your own way. Make yourself unique and be real.

That Mr. A used a method and it works does not mean that Mr. B will succeed when he use Mr. A's method. Be yourself and be original.

10. LOVE YOURSELF

Do you know that the number one enemy of progress you
have is you? Yes, you are your own enemy. Why? Because
you hate yourself. You don't love yourself.

You hate yourself for being short, for coming from a poor
family, for being black skinned etc. You are so naive that
you forget that all these does not count.

You procrastinate a lot. Instead of sticking to a particular
goal and achieving it gradually, you quit at the very start of
the plan.

Love yourself, believe in yourself for you are a special
being.

11. LOVE WHAT YOU DO — PASSION

You can never be successful if you don't love what you do.
A lot of people do not have passion for their career.
Maybe because your parents forced you into that career or
probably the situation of the present society. Or maybe

you moved into that career just for monetary gains, you will never achieve something.

The reason I'm a writer is not just because it is my talent, but because I love writing. It's my passion. Despite being multi talented, there's no way I can choose all my talents as a career. I only choose the ones I'm more passionate about.

If you are passionate about Football go ahead with it, if you love writing venture into it, and you'll see yourself succeeding.

12. LEARN TO FORGIVE

Its hard to forgive someone. Yes, especially when your offender has done something that has hurt you so badly. But even at that, learn to forgive.

You may not know that forgiveness paves way for a Man's success. You should not hold grudges for a long time. It decays the heart, you know.

Try to forgive your offenders and free yourself from

holding grudge that will cause you heart decay.

13. HAVE FUN

"All work and no play makes jack a dull boy..."

Don't kill yourself with work in the process of trying to be hardworking. Always have fun even as you do your work. You have fun to ease off stress and be vibrant in your subsequent work.

Have fun to make yourself feel good. Don't get pissed with work for it may cause you a lot of psychological trauma.

14. GIVE TO PEOPLE

Dear reader, i'm quite sure you must have have heard the sage 'givers never lack' which is absolutely true. You can never lack when you give to people.

Giving does not only include money. You can give advice,

you can give helpful tips, you can give life changing values and so on. They are all part of giving.

Hey, but don't give out something if you know you'll later regret giving it out. Giving should come from your heart.

15. VALUE CORRECTION

This is another mystery of success. Don't feel bad when you are being corrected for something you are not dong properly. Everybody makes mistake. We are fallible and should accept correction when one is pointed out.

Even if the correction comes as a chastisement or criticism, don't bother about it.

16. NEVER PROMISE WHAT YOU WON'T DO

You need to stop this promise and fail attitude if you really want to go far in life. It will bring you down and can slow your pace into success.

Why should you promise what you are not sure you would do. Instead of making promises that you can't keep, don't even bother making such promises.

People will loose trust in you if you continue to promise and fail them. And you know what that means; they'll find it hard to ever trust you again. They'll see you as one who does not keep his word.

So try not to make promises that you can't keep.

17. DON'T SPEND EXTRAVAGANTLY

If you continue spending more than necessary, you can drastically reduce to nothing. Make wise use of your money. Don't just spend excessively just because you have money. " vanity upon vanity, all is vanity..."

Hey,don't get it twisted. I'm not saying you should not enjoy your money. Hell no! You made the money you want so you are free to enjoy as you want.

You can even buy your country if you want. Lol..I'm kidding.

Just make wise use of your money,Simple. Invest them instead of just spending.

18. READ A LOT

Hey, if you are not a reading type, you have to develope that habit. Reading will help you grow mentally and intellectually.

You can read anyway. You can read news, blog posts, novels, self improvement books, health tips, life lessons and the rest.

By reading, you expand your knowledge and then more ideas come to your mind.

19. LOVE TRAVEL

Do you know that you can become successful by travelling? Yes, it is another mystery of success you should know. When you travel, you get ideas of places and you get to know many things you are not aware of.

You see many successful people in different places and you discover their strategies of getting to the top. You can gain new contacts and new ideas from your tour experience.

20. USE THE LUR FORMULA

Have you heard of the LUR formula? The LUR formula is another mystery of success. LUR is an acronym which stands for;

L — Learn

U — Unlearn

R — Relearn

Learn skills that will help you grow. Memorise helpful tips and let them stick to you.

Unlearn all the negative attitudes. Let go of those negative thoughts that bring you down.

21. BE COMMITTED

Commitment according to the advanced oxford learners dictionary is the willingness to work hard and give your energy and time to a job or an activity.

Successful people are always committed to their work. They put all their efforts to make sure they succeed.

Always be commited in what you do and you see yourself soaring higher.

22. SEEK ADVICE FROM RESPONSIBLE PEOPLE

I must say that there is nobody in the world who does not need advice. Let's say a secondary school leaver wants to further to the university and during the university tertiary matriculation examination (utme) preparation, he is expected to seek advice from people who have had such experience.

Maybe you are into a business or you have a problem, you need responsible people to advise you on how to solve such problem. In that way, you are climbing to greatness.

23. X-RAY YOUR BEHAVIOR

An x-ray is used in the medical field to view the internal structures of the body.

As you go on with your day to day activities, always xray your behaviour. Pause for a moment and take a view of how you behave, or your attitude towards people or things that comes your way.

Unlearn any bad behaviour you noticed and replace them with good ones.

24. STOP THE BLAME

Do you keep blaming people each time you fail? Or do you keep blaming things and circumstances around you? If you still have this 'I blame' attitude, just stop it for it won't take you anywhere.

We need to accept that we won't always make the right decisions, that we'll screw up royally sometimes — understanding that failure is not the opposite of success,it's part of success.

25. PUT OUT FEAR

A lot of people have not yet achieved their goals because of fear. Fear is a killer of ones destiny. You can never succeed if you have it in you.

You are afraid of what people will say if you take certain actions. You fear criticism. You are afraid you won't get more customers. You are afraid your market won't sell.

Be not afraid. Take up courage and fight that battle. Its your fight and you must fight it.

26. BE SACRIFICIAL

Do you know that it takes sacrifice to be successful? Mention any successful person in the world who never sacrificed. There is absolutely none.

Sacrifice in this aspect is not connected to anything ritual. You sacrifice what its hard to give out. Sacrifice your time, your money, name it.

Sacrifice does a lot of wonders in making one successful.

27. GET A MENTOR

Having a mentor or coach to guide you in your area of specialization helps pull you to success. You need a mentor or a coach to teach you some vital things you need to know.

They are always there to guide you to avoid errors.

Mentors are elevators to success. Without them, I must say you'll be left confused and you'll keep struggling at a particular level you should have surpassed.

28. WORRY LESS

Worry brings a man down both physically, mentally and psychologically. You have to worry less if you want to attain success.

I remember **' Hakuna matata '** a word I heard from **The lion king**, a popular kid movie. It means 'no worry'

So, always keep away from worrying too much. It is a silent killer, therefore always avoid it.

29. BE CONSISTENT

Consistency is the quality of having the same opinion, standard and belief.

It is one of the mystery of success which made many successful.

In whatever you do, always be consistent. Keep sharing that product, keep advertising yourself. Don't look at what people will say.

Be consistent and you'll see yourself get bigger everyday.

30. PRAY FERVENTLY

I purposely mentioned this as the number 30 mystery of success. It should have been the first but I just wanted to end this book with it.

This is an umbrella which covers all other mysteries of success, including those not mentioned in this book. Prayer opens a way for your success.

Always pray without ceasing and you'll see great things continue to happen. Crown your prayer with belief, faith and daily affirmations. Declare good things in your life as you pray fervently. Don't doubt what you just prayed for. It must surely come to pass.

Here comes the end of the 30 mystery of success. May all your expectations be granted as you strive for success.

Remain blessed.

www.ingramcontent.com/pod-product-compliance
Lightning Source LLC
Chambersburg PA
CBHW040949110726
48006CB00007B/1326